Feathered & **FURRY** friends

Shanda Cameron
Illustrated by:
Danielle Shreenan

With love for, Will & Jesse.

Shanda Cameron

Danielle Shreenan

Every morning Miss Molly
checks on her feathered and furry friends.

The chickadees are already looking for the special
seeds Miss Molly will put in their feeder.

The little squirrel is tucked into position waiting
for the sunflower seeds she places on the deck.

The crow has landed in her favourite tree watching for
the piece of bread she knows has been saved for her.

Two little bunnies peek out from under the bush looking
for the carrots that taste so sweet.

Mommy raccoon sees the small biscuit that she will
wash before she eats and feeds to her babies.

A little fox appears, drooling, knowing how
tasty her piece of meat will taste.

A cute little skunk steps onto the deck knowing that no
one will stop her from eating the berries put out for her.

A small stray cat comes for her dish of food that
she looks soooo forward to every morning.

Miss Molly knows who her last visitor will be. A beautiful deer
with her newborn fawn. They love to eat the apples
that are cut into pieces for them.

Miss Molly's dog Kiwi sits patiently, hoping there's
a special treat for her. Of course there is!

Standing on her deck Miss Molly tells them all that she will see them again tomorrow and knows that her feathered and furry friends are very happy.

AuthorHouse™
1663 Liberty Drive
Bloomington, IN 47403
www.authorhouse.com
Phone: 1-800-839-8640

First published by AuthorHouse 8/23/2010

ISBN: 978-1-4520-6909-8 (sc)

Library of Congress Control Number: 2010912361

Printed in the United States of America

This book is printed on acid-free paper.

authorHOUSE®

LaVergne, TN USA
21 September 2010
197943LV00002B

9781452069098